The Teacher's Big Planbook

This planbook belongs to:

Name _____

Grade _____

Room _____

School _____

Year _____

Telephone _____

Contents

Student Information 2-3

Conferences 4

Substitute Information 5

Seating Plan 6

Birthdays 7

Student Medical Information 8

Student Transportation Information 9

Daily Schedule 10

Yearly Planning 11

Planning Pages 12-95

Notes 96

© Carson-Dellosa CD-8205

Student Information

Student	Parent/Guardian	Address	Home Phone	Work Phone

© Carson-Dellosa CD-8205

Student Information

Student	Parent/Guardian	Address	Home Phone	Work Phone

Conferences

Student	Contact	Date	Notes

Birthdays

January	February	March	April

May	June	July	August

September	October	November	December

Student Medical Information

Student	Allergies	Daily Medications	Emergency Contact	Phone

Student Transportation Information

Bus Riders	Bus #	Car Riders	Walkers	Other

Daily Schedule

Monday	Tuesday	Wednesday	Thursday	Friday

© Carson-Dellosa CD-8205

Yearly Planning 2023

January
January 23 2:00PM FILLINGS

February

March

April
D.O
Dr Beauregard 10:30 28th
Walters Dentistry 18th 2:30 PM

May

June

July

August

September

October

November

December

	Subject							
	Time							

Monday _____

Absences: _____

_____

Extra Duties: _____

Reminders: _____

Tuesday _____

Absences: _____

_____

Extra Duties: _____

Reminders: _____

Wednesday _____

Absences: _____

_____

Extra Duties: _____

Reminders: _____

Thursday _____

Absences: _____

_____

Extra Duties: _____

Reminders: _____

Friday _____

Absences: _____

_____

Extra Duties: _____

Reminders: _____

© Carson-Dellosa CD-8205

	Subject							
	Time							

Monday _____

Absences: _____

Extra Duties: _____

Reminders: _____

Tuesday _____

Absences: _____

Extra Duties: _____

Reminders: _____

Wednesday _____

Absences: _____

Extra Duties: _____

Reminders: _____

Thursday _____

Absences: _____

Extra Duties: _____

Reminders: _____

Friday _____

Absences: _____

Extra Duties: _____

Reminders: _____

	Subject							
	Time							

Monday _____

Absences: _____

Extra Duties: _____

Reminders: _____

Tuesday _____

Absences: _____

Extra Duties: _____

Reminders: _____

Wednesday _____

Absences: _____

Extra Duties: _____

Reminders: _____

Thursday _____

Absences: _____

Extra Duties: _____

Reminders: _____

Friday _____

Absences: _____

Extra Duties: _____

Reminders: _____

© Carson-Dellosa CD-8205

	Subject							
	Time							

Monday
Absences: _____

Extra Duties: _____
Reminders: _____

Tuesday
Absences: _____

Extra Duties: _____
Reminders: _____

Wednesday
Absences: _____

Extra Duties: _____
Reminders: _____

Thursday
Absences: _____

Extra Duties: _____
Reminders: _____

Friday
Absences: _____

Extra Duties: _____
Reminders: _____

© Carson-Dellosa CD-8205

	Subject								
	Time								

Monday
Absences: _____

Extra Duties: _____
Reminders: _____

Tuesday
Absences: _____

Extra Duties: _____
Reminders: _____

Wednesday
Absences: _____

Extra Duties: _____
Reminders: _____

Thursday
Absences: _____

Extra Duties: _____
Reminders: _____

Friday
Absences: _____

Extra Duties: _____
Reminders: _____

© Carson-Dellosa CD-8205

	Subject							
	Time							

Monday
Absences: _____

Extra Duties: _____
Reminders: _____

Tuesday
Absences: _____

Extra Duties: _____
Reminders: _____

Wednesday
Absences: _____

Extra Duties: _____
Reminders: _____

Thursday
Absences: _____

Extra Duties: _____
Reminders: _____

Friday
Absences: _____

Extra Duties: _____
Reminders: _____

	Subject							
	Time							
Monday Absences: Extra Duties: Reminders:								
Tuesday Absences: Extra Duties: Reminders:								
Wednesday Absences: Extra Duties: Reminders:								
Thursday Absences: Extra Duties: Reminders:								
Friday Absences: Extra Duties: Reminders:								

	Subject							
	Time							

Monday

Absences: _____

_____

Extra Duties: _____

Reminders: _____

Tuesday

Absences: _____

_____

Extra Duties: _____

Reminders: _____

Wednesday

Absences: _____

_____

Extra Duties: _____

Reminders: _____

Thursday

Absences: _____

_____

Extra Duties: _____

Reminders: _____

Friday

Absences: _____

_____

Extra Duties: _____

Reminders: _____

	Subject								
	Time								
Monday _____ Absences: _____ Extra Duties: _____ Reminders: _____									
Tuesday _____ Absences: _____ Extra Duties: _____ Reminders: _____									
Wednesday _____ Absences: _____ Extra Duties: _____ Reminders: _____									
Thursday _____ Absences: _____ Extra Duties: _____ Reminders: _____									
Friday _____ Absences: _____ Extra Duties: _____ Reminders: _____									

	Subject							
	Time							

Monday

Absences:

Extra Duties:

Reminders:

Tuesday

Absences:

Extra Duties:

Reminders:

Wednesday

Absences:

Extra Duties:

Reminders:

Thursday

Absences:

Extra Duties:

Reminders:

Friday

Absences:

Extra Duties:

Reminders:

	Subject							
	Time							

Monday _____

Absences: _____

Extra Duties: _____

Reminders: _____

Tuesday _____

Absences: _____

Extra Duties: _____

Reminders: _____

Wednesday _____

Absences: _____

Extra Duties: _____

Reminders: _____

Thursday _____

Absences: _____

Extra Duties: _____

Reminders: _____

Friday _____

Absences: _____

Extra Duties: _____

Reminders: _____

	Subject								
	Time								

Monday
Absences: _____

Extra Duties: _____
Reminders: _____

Tuesday
Absences: _____

Extra Duties: _____
Reminders: _____

Wednesday
Absences: _____

Extra Duties: _____
Reminders: _____

Thursday
Absences: _____

Extra Duties: _____
Reminders: _____

Friday
Absences: _____

Extra Duties: _____
Reminders: _____

© Carson-Dellosa CD-8205

	Subject								
	Time								

Monday
Absences: _____

Extra Duties: _____
Reminders: _____

Tuesday
Absences: _____

Extra Duties: _____
Reminders: _____

Wednesday
Absences: _____

Extra Duties: _____
Reminders: _____

Thursday
Absences: _____

Extra Duties: _____
Reminders: _____

Friday
Absences: _____

Extra Duties: _____
Reminders: _____

	Subject							
	Time							

Monday
Absences: _____

Extra Duties: _____
Reminders: _____

Tuesday
Absences: _____

Extra Duties: _____
Reminders: _____

Wednesday
Absences: _____

Extra Duties: _____
Reminders: _____

Thursday
Absences: _____

Extra Duties: _____
Reminders: _____

Friday
Absences: _____

Extra Duties: _____
Reminders: _____

	Subject								
	Time								

Monday _____
Absences: _____

Extra Duties: _____
Reminders: _____

Tuesday _____
Absences: _____

Extra Duties: _____
Reminders: _____

Wednesday _____
Absences: _____

Extra Duties: _____
Reminders: _____

Thursday _____
Absences: _____

Extra Duties: _____
Reminders: _____

Friday _____
Absences: _____

Extra Duties: _____
Reminders: _____

© Carson-Dellosa CD-8205

	Subject								
	Time								

Monday

Absences:

Extra Duties:

Reminders:

Tuesday

Absences:

Extra Duties:

Reminders:

Wednesday

Absences:

Extra Duties:

Reminders:

Thursday

Absences:

Extra Duties:

Reminders:

Friday

Absences:

Extra Duties:

Reminders:

© Carson-Dellosa CD-8205

	Subject								
	Time								
Monday									
Absences:									
Extra Duties:									
Reminders:									
Tuesday									
Absences:									
Extra Duties:									
Reminders:									
Wednesday									
Absences:									
Extra Duties:									
Reminders:									
Thursday									
Absences:									
Extra Duties:									
Reminders:									
Friday									
Absences:									
Extra Duties:									
Reminders:									

	Subject							
	Time							

Monday
Absences:

Extra Duties:

Reminders:

Tuesday
Absences:

Extra Duties:

Reminders:

Wednesday
Absences:

Extra Duties:

Reminders:

Thursday
Absences:

Extra Duties:

Reminders:

Friday
Absences:

Extra Duties:

Reminders:

	Subject							
	Time							

Monday

Absences: _____

Extra Duties: _____
Reminders: _____

Tuesday

Absences: _____

Extra Duties: _____
Reminders: _____

Wednesday

Absences: _____

Extra Duties: _____
Reminders: _____

Thursday

Absences: _____

Extra Duties: _____
Reminders: _____

Friday

Absences: _____

Extra Duties: _____
Reminders: _____

	Subject							
	Time							
Monday _____ Absences: _____ _____ Extra Duties: _____ Reminders: _____								
Tuesday _____ Absences: _____ _____ Extra Duties: _____ Reminders: _____								
Wednesday _____ Absences: _____ _____ Extra Duties: _____ Reminders: _____								
Thursday _____ Absences: _____ _____ Extra Duties: _____ Reminders: _____								
Friday _____ Absences: _____ _____ Extra Duties: _____ Reminders: _____								

	Subject							
	Time							

Monday
Absences: _____

Extra Duties: _____
Reminders: _____

Tuesday
Absences: _____

Extra Duties: _____
Reminders: _____

Wednesday
Absences: _____

Extra Duties: _____
Reminders: _____

Thursday
Absences: _____

Extra Duties: _____
Reminders: _____

Friday
Absences: _____

Extra Duties: _____
Reminders: _____

	Subject								
	Time								

Monday
Absences: _____

Extra Duties: _____
Reminders: _____

Tuesday
Absences: _____

Extra Duties: _____
Reminders: _____

Wednesday
Absences: _____

Extra Duties: _____
Reminders: _____

Thursday
Absences: _____

Extra Duties: _____
Reminders: _____

Friday
Absences: _____

Extra Duties: _____
Reminders: _____

© Carson-Dellosa CD-8205

	Subject							
	Time							

Monday
Absences:

Extra Duties:

Reminders:

Tuesday
Absences:

Extra Duties:

Reminders:

Wednesday
Absences:

Extra Duties:

Reminders:

Thursday
Absences:

Extra Duties:

Reminders:

Friday
Absences:

Extra Duties:

Reminders:

© Carson-Dellosa CD-8205

	Subject								
	Time								

Monday _____

Absences: _____

Extra Duties: _____

Reminders: _____

Tuesday _____

Absences: _____

Extra Duties: _____

Reminders: _____

Wednesday _____

Absences: _____

Extra Duties: _____

Reminders: _____

Thursday _____

Absences: _____

Extra Duties: _____

Reminders: _____

Friday _____

Absences: _____

Extra Duties: _____

Reminders: _____

	Subject								
	Time								

Monday _____

Absences: _____

Extra Duties: _____

Reminders: _____

Tuesday _____

Absences: _____

Extra Duties: _____

Reminders: _____

Wednesday _____

Absences: _____

Extra Duties: _____

Reminders: _____

Thursday _____

Absences: _____

Extra Duties: _____

Reminders: _____

Friday _____

Absences: _____

Extra Duties: _____

Reminders: _____

	Subject									
	Time									

Monday _____

Absences: _____

Extra Duties: _____

Reminders: _____

Tuesday _____

Absences: _____

Extra Duties: _____

Reminders: _____

Wednesday _____

Absences: _____

Extra Duties: _____

Reminders: _____

Thursday _____

Absences: _____

Extra Duties: _____

Reminders: _____

Friday _____

Absences: _____

Extra Duties: _____

Reminders: _____

	Subject								
	Time								

Monday _____

Absences: _____
_____

Extra Duties: _____
Reminders: _____

Tuesday _____

Absences: _____
_____

Extra Duties: _____
Reminders: _____

Wednesday _____

Absences: _____
_____

Extra Duties: _____
Reminders: _____

Thursday _____

Absences: _____
_____

Extra Duties: _____
Reminders: _____

Friday _____

Absences: _____
_____

Extra Duties: _____
Reminders: _____

	Subject								
	Time								

Monday _____

Absences: _____

_____

Extra Duties: _____

Reminders: _____

_____

Tuesday _____

Absences: _____

_____

Extra Duties: _____

Reminders: _____

_____

Wednesday _____

Absences: _____

_____

Extra Duties: _____

Reminders: _____

_____

Thursday _____

Absences: _____

_____

Extra Duties: _____

Reminders: _____

_____

Friday _____

Absences: _____

_____

Extra Duties: _____

Reminders: _____

_____

© Carson-Dellosa CD-8205

67

	Subject							
	Time							

Monday

Absences: _____

Extra Duties: _____
Reminders: _____

Tuesday

Absences: _____

Extra Duties: _____
Reminders: _____

Wednesday

Absences: _____

Extra Duties: _____
Reminders: _____

Thursday

Absences: _____

Extra Duties: _____
Reminders: _____

Friday

Absences: _____

Extra Duties: _____
Reminders: _____

	Subject								
	Time								

Monday
Absences:

Extra Duties:

Reminders:

Tuesday
Absences:

Extra Duties:

Reminders:

Wednesday
Absences:

Extra Duties:

Reminders:

Thursday
Absences:

Extra Duties:

Reminders:

Friday
Absences:

Extra Duties:

Reminders:

	Subject							
	Time							

Monday _____

Absences: _____

Extra Duties: _____

Reminders: _____

Tuesday _____

Absences: _____

Extra Duties: _____

Reminders: _____

Wednesday _____

Absences: _____

Extra Duties: _____

Reminders: _____

Thursday _____

Absences: _____

Extra Duties: _____

Reminders: _____

Friday _____

Absences: _____

Extra Duties: _____

Reminders: _____

© Carson-Dellosa CD-8205

	Subject							
	Time							

Monday
Absences:

Extra Duties:
Reminders:

Tuesday
Absences:

Extra Duties:
Reminders:

Wednesday
Absences:

Extra Duties:
Reminders:

Thursday
Absences:

Extra Duties:
Reminders:

Friday
Absences:

Extra Duties:
Reminders:

	Subject							
	Time							

Monday

Absences: _____

Extra Duties: _____

Reminders: _____

Tuesday

Absences: _____

Extra Duties: _____

Reminders: _____

Wednesday

Absences: _____

Extra Duties: _____

Reminders: _____

Thursday

Absences: _____

Extra Duties: _____

Reminders: _____

Friday

Absences: _____

Extra Duties: _____

Reminders: _____

	Subject							
	Time							

Monday
Absences: _____

Extra Duties: _____
Reminders: _____

Tuesday
Absences: _____

Extra Duties: _____
Reminders: _____

Wednesday
Absences: _____

Extra Duties: _____
Reminders: _____

Thursday
Absences: _____

Extra Duties: _____
Reminders: _____

Friday
Absences: _____

Extra Duties: _____
Reminders: _____

© Carson-Dellosa CD-8205

	Subject								
	Time								
Monday										
Absences:										
Extra Duties:										
Reminders:										
Tuesday										
Absences:										
Extra Duties:										
Reminders:										
Wednesday										
Absences:										
Extra Duties:										
Reminders:										
Thursday										
Absences:										
Extra Duties:										
Reminders:										
Friday										
Absences:										
Extra Duties:										
Reminders:										

© Carson-Dellosa CD-8205

	Subject								
	Time								

Monday _____

Absences:

Extra Duties:

Reminders:

Tuesday _____

Absences:

Extra Duties:

Reminders:

Wednesday _____

Absences:

Extra Duties:

Reminders:

Thursday _____

Absences:

Extra Duties:

Reminders:

Friday _____

Absences:

Extra Duties:

Reminders:

© Carson-Dellosa CD-8205

	Subject								
	Time								

Monday
Absences:

Extra Duties:
Reminders:

Tuesday
Absences:

Extra Duties:
Reminders:

Wednesday
Absences:

Extra Duties:
Reminders:

Thursday
Absences:

Extra Duties:
Reminders:

Friday
Absences:

Extra Duties:
Reminders:

© Carson-Dellosa CD-8205

	Subject								
	Time								

Monday _____

Absences: _____

Extra Duties: _____

Reminders: _____

Tuesday _____

Absences: _____

Extra Duties: _____

Reminders: _____

Wednesday _____

Absences: _____

Extra Duties: _____

Reminders: _____

Thursday _____

Absences: _____

Extra Duties: _____

Reminders: _____

Friday _____

Absences: _____

Extra Duties: _____

Reminders: _____

© Carson-Dellosa CD-820

	Subject							
	Time							

Monday _____

Absences: _____

Extra Duties: _____

Reminders: _____

Tuesday _____

Absences: _____

Extra Duties: _____

Reminders: _____

Wednesday _____

Absences: _____

Extra Duties: _____

Reminders: _____

Thursday _____

Absences: _____

Extra Duties: _____

Reminders: _____

Friday _____

Absences: _____

Extra Duties: _____

Reminders: _____

	Subject								
	Time								

Monday
Absences:

Extra Duties:
Reminders:

Tuesday
Absences:

Extra Duties:
Reminders:

Wednesday
Absences:

Extra Duties:
Reminders:

Thursday
Absences:

Extra Duties:
Reminders:

Friday
Absences:

Extra Duties:
Reminders:

© Carson-Dellosa CD-8205

Notes